Fun Facts about Carbon

Chemistry for Kids

The Element Series

Children's Chemistry Books

BABY PROFESSOR

EDUCATION KIDS

Speedy Publishing LLC
40 E. Main St. #1156
Newark, DE 19711
www.speedypublishing.com

Being one of the greatest significant elements to sustain life on Earth, Carbon is the basis for animal and plant life. It is considered as the fourth most ample element and is second in our human body. In this book, we are going to discuss its properties and characteristics as well as how it came to become such a useful element.

CHARACTERISTICS AND PROPERTIES OF CARBON

Carbon is continually cycled throughout our plant life, animal life, oceans, and atmosphere. We general refer to life on Earth as a "carbon-based life."

Antoine Lavoisier

Characteristics and Properties

While it has been around since ancient times, in 1772 a French scientist by the name of Antoine Lavoisier discovered that diamond was made of carbon.

The word carbon comes from the Latin word "carbo" which means charcoal or coal. Carbon is an element is noted with the symbol C and atomic number 6. Its atomic weight is 12.011 and is considered a non-metal. When at room temperature it becomes a solid. The melting point for the diamond is 3550 degrees Celsius or 6442 degrees Fahrenheit. Its boiling point is 4200 degrees Celsius or 7600 degrees Fahrenheit. Graphite becomes sublime at 3642 degrees Celsius and 6588 degrees Fahrenheit.

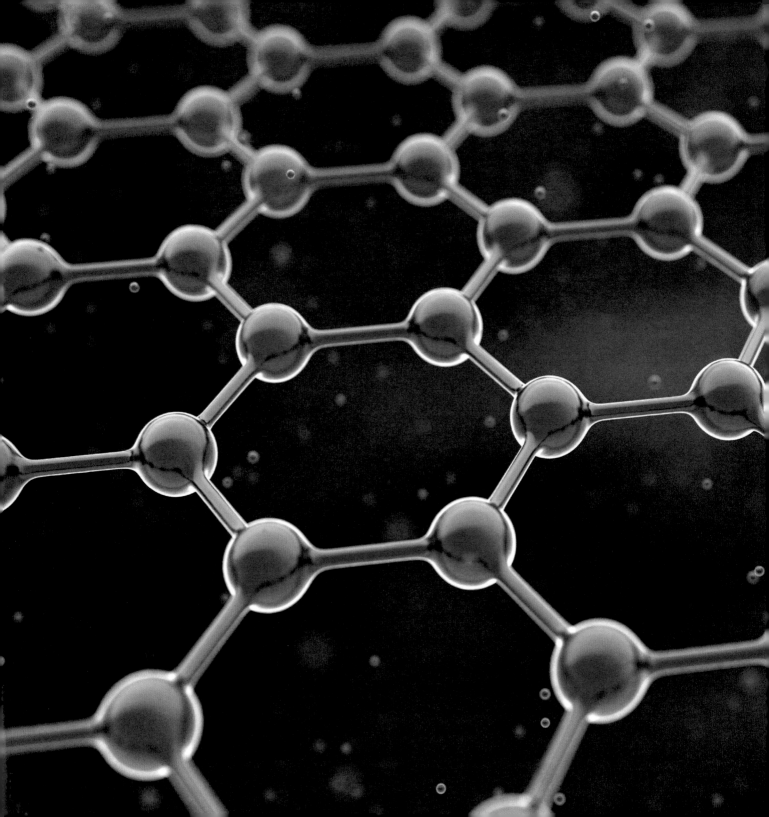

When an element configures itself in a way to change its properties and structures, the result is known as allotropes. Since carbon can form four bonds, it contains several different allotropes that each contain their own distinguished properties and uses. It is made up of three allotropes including graphite, amorphous, and diamond and they can be found on Earth. Made from similar elements, allotropes' atoms come together in a different way. Each carbon allotrope contains physical properties that are different.

The hardest substance found in nature is carbon in its diamond allotrope. It contains the greatest thermal conductivity of any element and is transparent in color. Graphite is found in a black-gray color and it is one of the softest materials. It is found to be a good conductor of electricity. Amorphous carbon is found to be black and known as soot and coal.

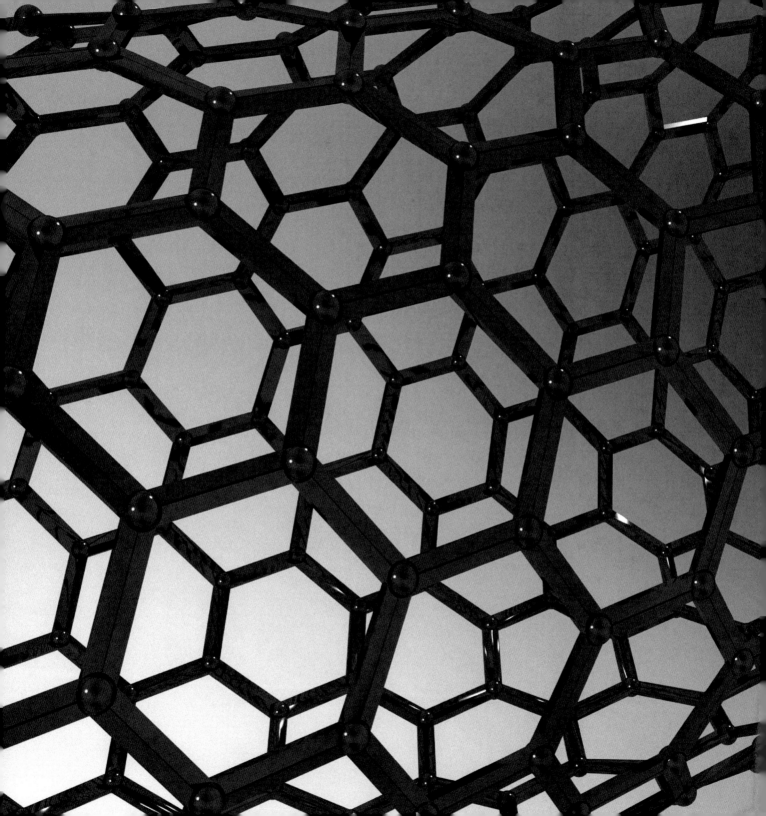

Carbon can create longer molecules chains by linking with different carbon atoms and is known to have the highest melting point of all elements.

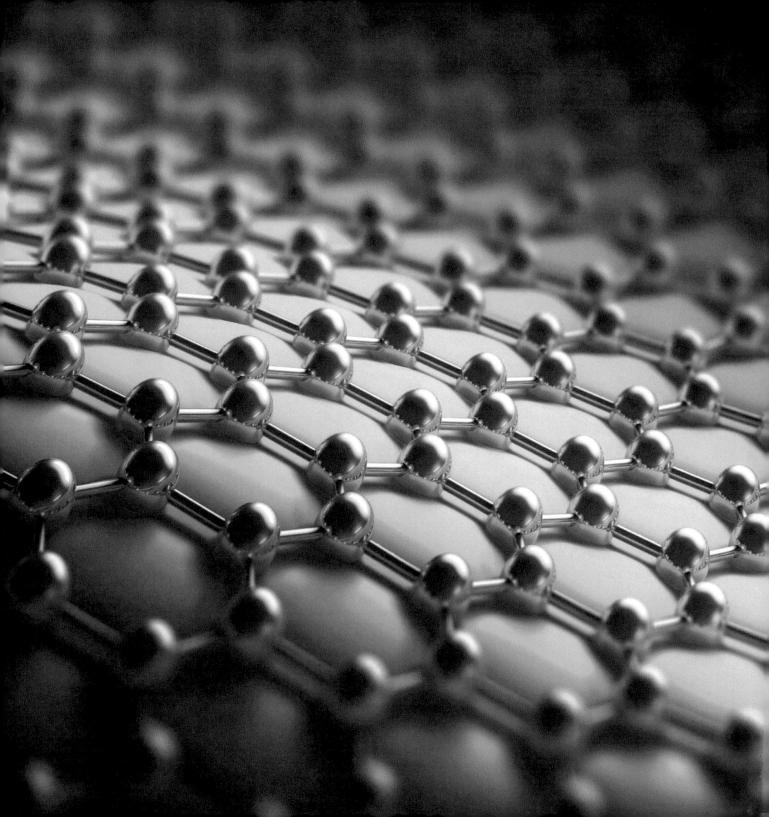

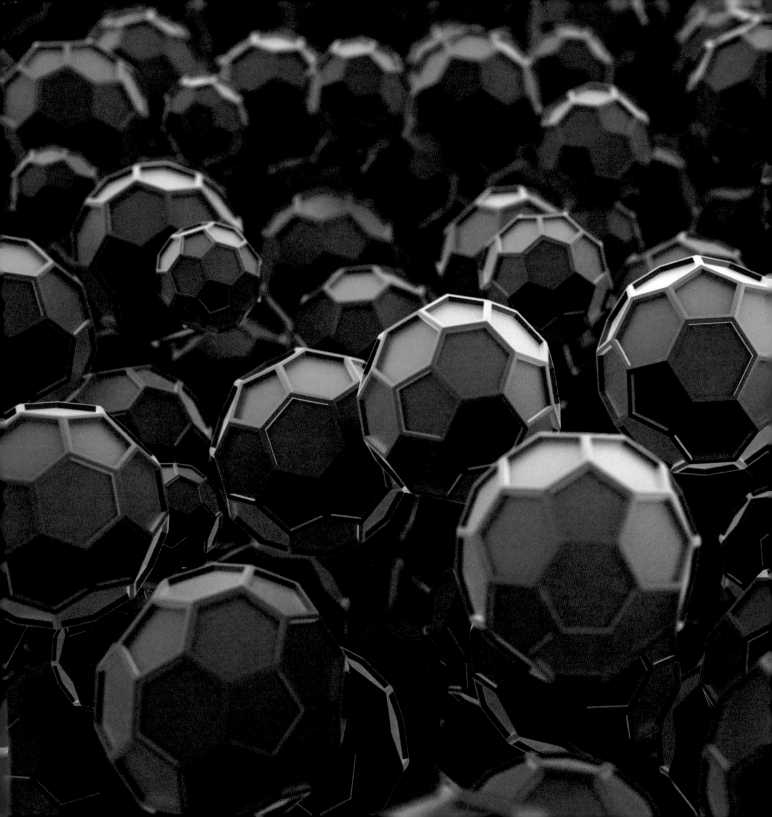

Recently, there was discovery of a fourth allotrope called fullerene which can form up to 10 million different compounds. It is also known as the building block of life due to its ability to bond with different non-metallic elements.

Carbon can be found anywhere on earth. Many rock formations, including limestone and marble, contain it as a major element. Compounds such as carbon dioxide in our atmosphere contain carbon and are dissolved in oceans and other large bodies of water. Hydrocarbons form fuels like coal, petroleum, and natural gas contain carbon. It is a part of all life forms. The human body is made up of 18% carbon mass.

Carbon is the fourth most abundant element in the universe and typically the fourth most abundant element in stars. Carbon stars are stars whose atmosphere has more carbon than oxygen.

Many organic molecules consist of chains or long rings of carbon atoms with additional atom elements attached. In addition to carbon, other well-known elements are oxygen, hydrogen, nitrogen, phosphorus, and sulfur.

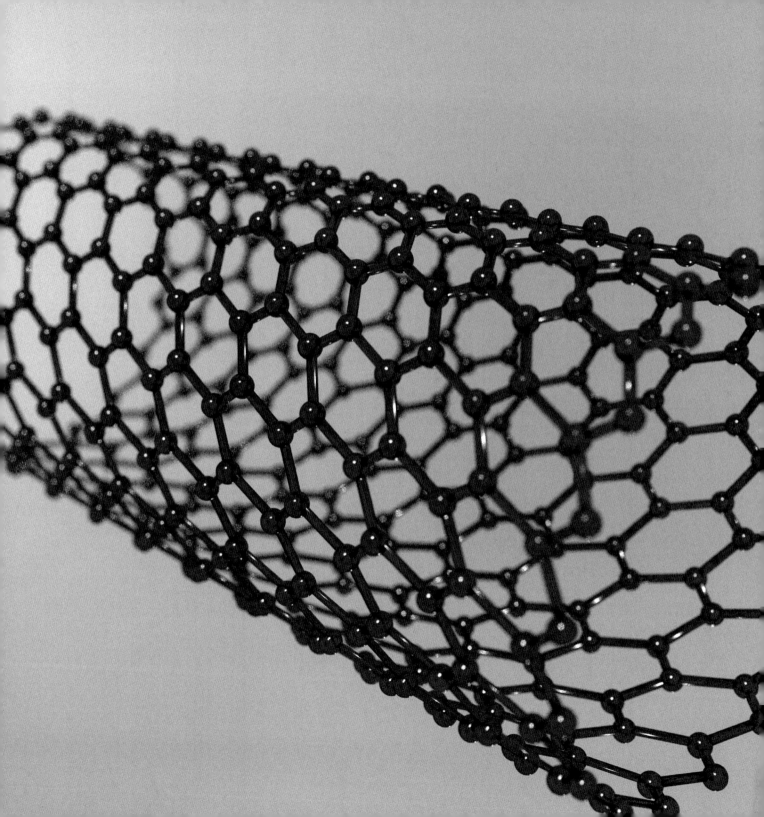

Hydrocarbons

Functional groups of organic compounds composed only of carbon and hydrogen atoms are known as hydrocarbons.

Hydrocarbons consist of other groups known to be alkanes. Alkanes consist of butane, ethane, methane, and propane. Some are used for cooking and heating. Other hydrocarbons are known as alkynes and alkenes.

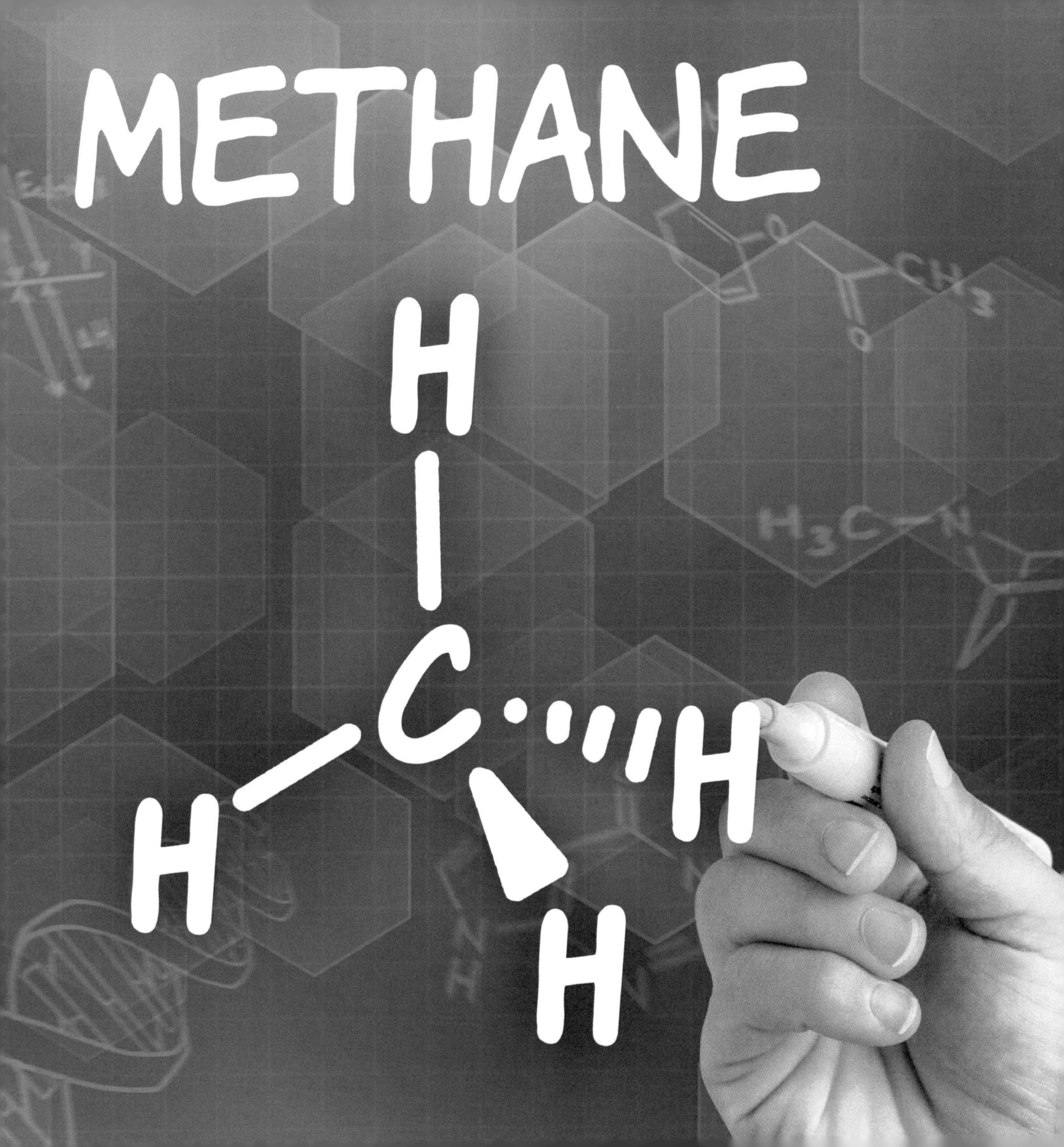
METHANE
H
C
H
H
H

Other Elements

Oxygen, nitrogen, boron, phosphorus, and sulfur form organic compounds when combined with carbon.

Carbon Monoxide

If there is not enough oxygen to make carbon dioxide, carbon monoxide forms and is very dangerous to animals and humans. Carbon monoxide is known to be the most prevalent type of fatal poisoning in different countries around the world. It is odorless and can be produced by cars. You should never leave your car on in your garage because you may die if you breathe too much of this gas.

The Carbon Cycle

Since its atoms are involved in the processes on our planet, they are always moving. Carbon is disbursed into the air and taken out by these processes. This cycle works closely with what is known as the oxygen cycle. Carbon sinks occur when nature removes carbon from the atmosphere.

While these processes remove carbon from our air, there are different processes that add it to the air and these are known as sources. With every breath, you turn oxygen into carbon dioxide. As animals and plants die, they decay and the carbon will either be stored in the ground as fossil fuels or released into the air. As we burn trees, plants, and fuel fossils, carbon is then released to the atmosphere.

CARBON CYCLE

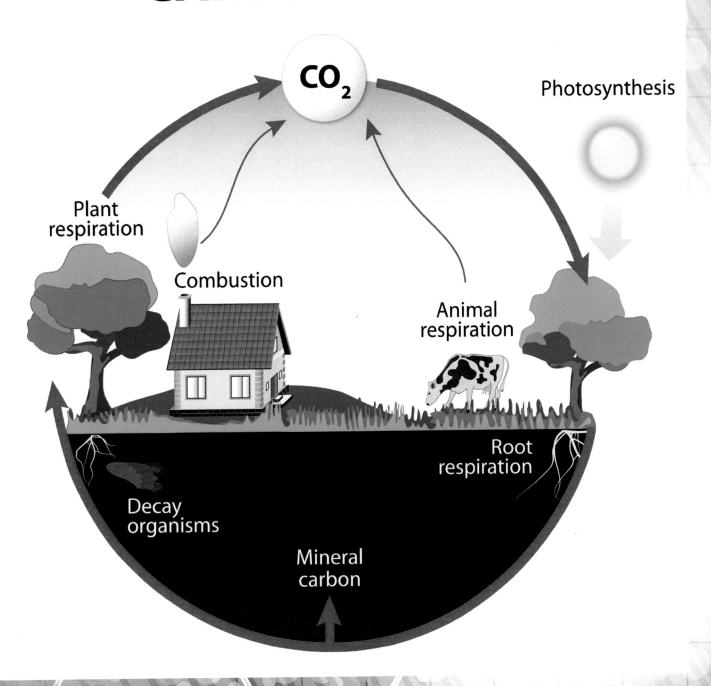

CO$_2$

Photosynthesis

Plant respiration

Combustion

Animal respiration

Decay organisms

Root respiration

Mineral carbon

Carbon Sinks

As discussed previously, carbon sinks remove carbon from the air. One example would be photosynthesis which is the process that plants use to grow. They utilize carbon dioxide, water, and sunlight and it turns into sugar and oxygen. Rainforests are a large area and removes a lot of it from the air.

The ocean is another example of a carbon sink. Sea water reacts with the carbon dioxide in our air and makes carbonic acid. Too much carbonic acid results in acid rain. While some acid rain is beneficial to create shells by sea organisms, too much of it is not good. These shells become sedimentary rock similar to limestone.

Nature does a magnificent job balancing the available carbon using the carbon cycle. The atmosphere also needs carbon to maintain the Earth's warm temperature.

How do we use it?

Most industries in the world use carbon in one way or another. Crude oil, coal, and methane gases use it for fuel. It can also be used to make different material including alloys and plastic.

While you may not realize it, carbon can be found in many everyday items that you use. The black used for painting and in printers is made from it. Graphite is used to make brakes, lubricants, and batteries, as well as the lead for pencils. Fine jewelry consisting of diamonds is a most valued gemstone, and is known for its hardness and can also be used in precision instruments and cutting tools. Deoxyribonucleic acid, known as DNA, is made up of complex molecules consisting of carbon chains. Among the many uses of DNA, it can be used for criminal investigations, paternity, and genetic disease.

Carbon Isotopes

Atoms containing the same number of protons and electrons, but the neutrons are different, are called isotopes. If you change the number of neutrons it will not change the element.

Carbon 12 consists of 6 neutrons and 6 protons, Carbon 13 consists of 7 neutrons and 6 protons, and Carbon 14 consists of 8 neutrons and 6 protons. As you may have guessed, the numbers in their titles were derived from adding the numbers of protons and neutrons. Since mass is derived from adding the number of protons and neutrons you might also realize that the difference of these isotopes is their mass.

Carbon-12 and carbon-13 are the two naturally occurring isotopes in carbon. The Earth is made up of about 99% of Carbon-12. Carbon dating is the term used to date carbon with Carbon-14. We know of 15 different carbon isotopes.

CARBON ATOM

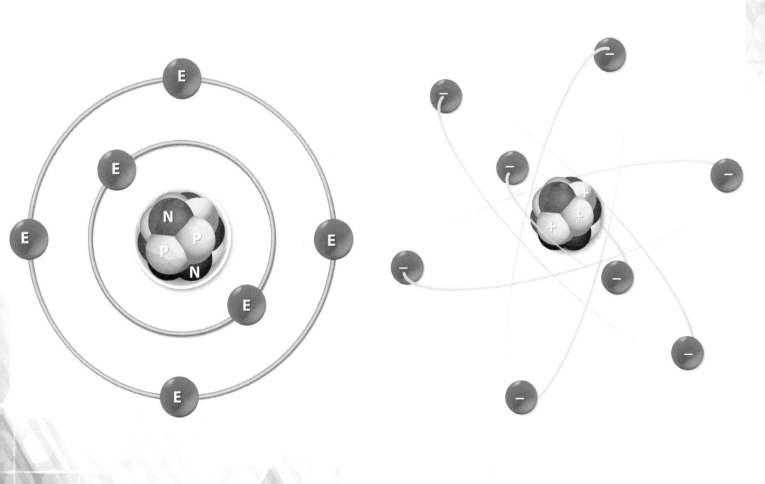

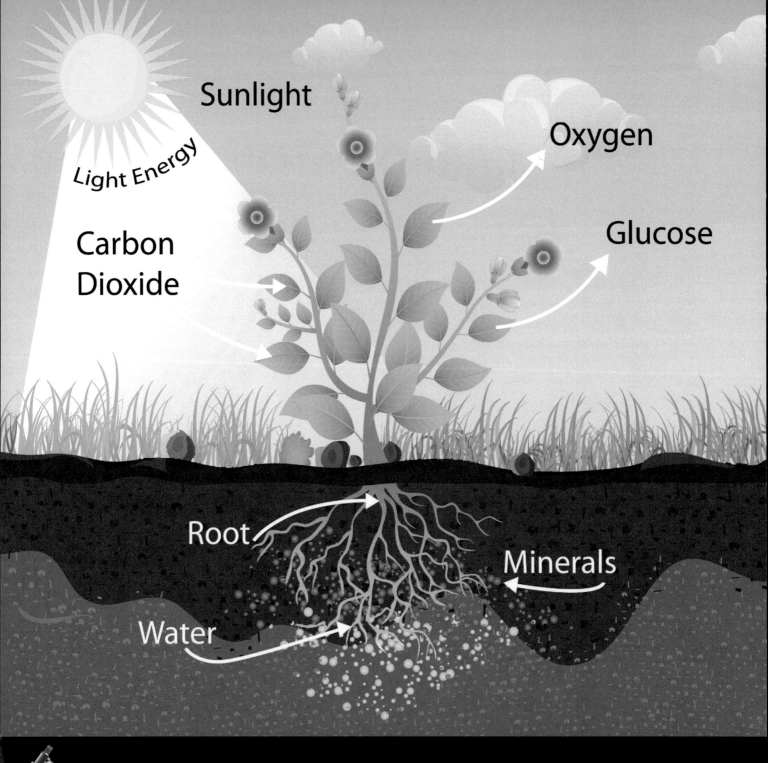

Sunlight

Light Energy

Carbon Dioxide

Oxygen

Glucose

Root

Minerals

Water

 Biology

Photosynthesis in Plan

Photosynthesis

Plants obtain carbon from the atmosphere through the process of photosynthesis. Photosynthesis consists of two words, "photo" which means light and "synthesis" which means to put together. Plants utilize sunlight for energy, water from rain, and carbon dioxide from breathing. Photosynthesis is the process of utilizing these three ingredients and making food. Since most plants can make food using this process, they do not need for it to be provided by animals or people.

Periodic Table of Elements

There is so much more to learn about this element as well as the many other elements. You may want to research the periodic table of elements which lists all the elements including their atomic structure. In 1869, a Russian chemist named Dmitri Mendeleev came up with this table. With the use of this table, he had the ability to predict properties of elements prior to them being discovered.

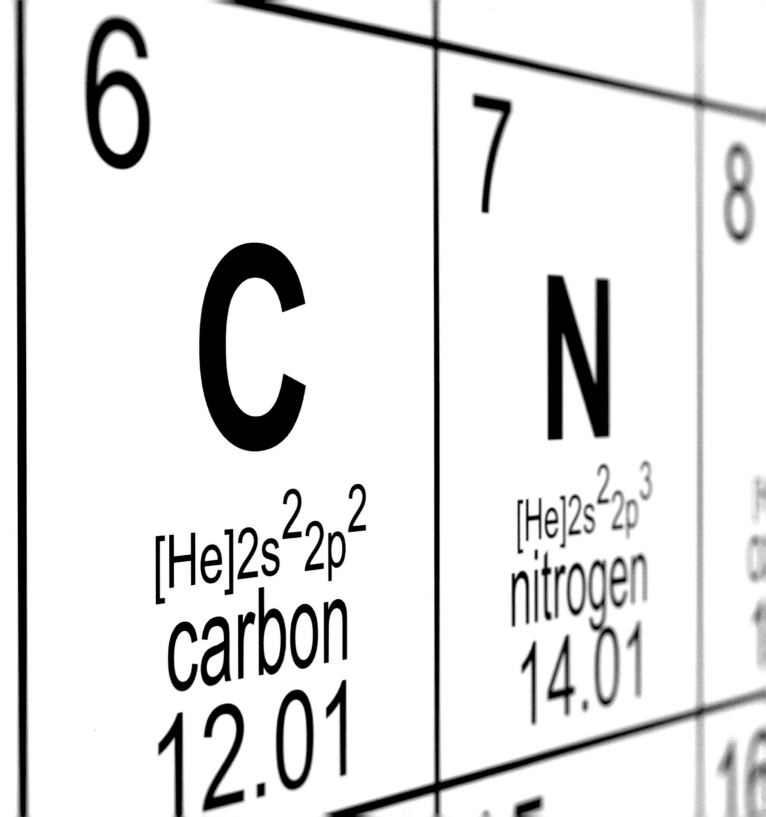

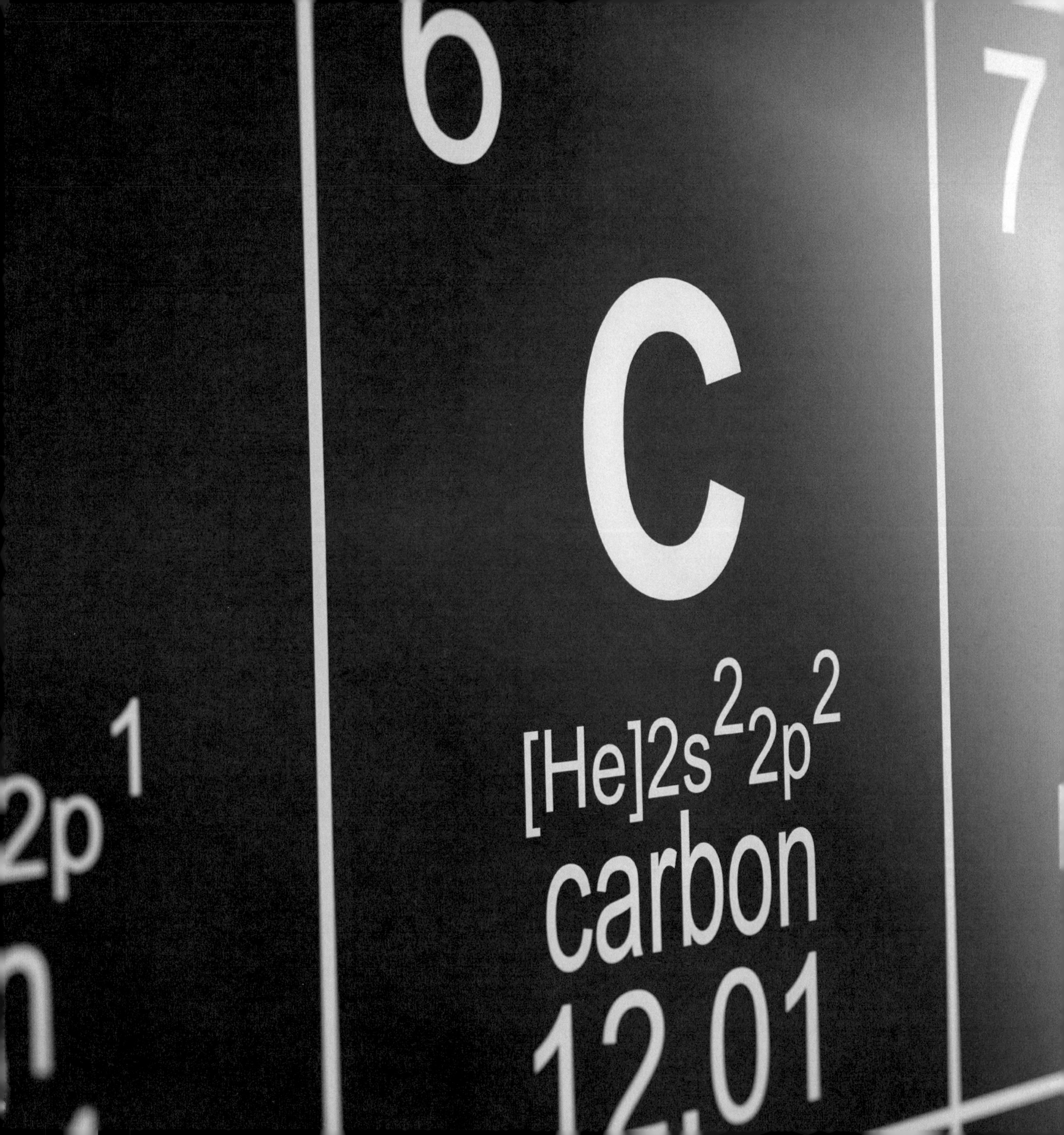

6

7

C

$[He]2s^2 2p^2$

carbon

12.01

2p

1

The table is divided into groups in order to assist chemists working with these elements to learn and predict how an element may behave or react in certain situations.

This table lists the name and abbreviation for each element. You may find some abbreviations easy to remember, such as H which is the abbreviation for hydrogen but some like iron (Fe) and gold (Au) are a somewhat more difficult to remember. In the instance of gold, "Au" originates from "aurum", which is the Latin word for gold.

					18
					2 4.002602 — 0 / 4.216 / (…) / 0.1787 — **He** / $1s^2$ / helium

13	14	15	16	17	18
5 10.811 — 3 / 4273 / 2352 / 2.34 — **B** / $[He]2s^22p^1$ / boron	**6** 12.0107 — 2,(±4) / 5100 / 4098 (sub.) / 2.62 — **C** / $[He]2s^22p^2$ / carbon	**7** 14.0067 — ±1,±2,(±3),4,5 / 77.4 / 63.29 / 1.2506 — **N** / $[He]2s^22p^3$ / nitrogen	**8** 15.9994 — -2 / 90.188 / 54.8 / 1.429 — **O** / $[He]2s^22p^4$ / oxygen	**9** 18.9984032 — -1 / 85.01 / 53.53 / 1.696 — **F** / $[He]2s^22p^5$ / fluorine	**10** 20.1797 — 0 / 27.102 / 24.48 / 0.8999 — **Ne** / $[He]2s^22p^6$ / neon
13 26.981538 — 3 / 2792 / 933.52 / 2.702 — **Al** / $[Ne]3s^23p^1$ / aluminum	**14** 28.0855 — 2,(4),−4 / 3538 / 1683 / 2.33 — **Si** / $[Ne]3s^23p^2$ / silicon	**15** 30.973761 — ±3,(5),7 / 550 / 317.3 / 1.82 — **P** / $[Ne]3s^23p^3$ / phosphorus	**16** 32.065 — ±2,4,(6) / 717.8 / 388.36 / 2.07 — **S** / $[Ne]3s^23p^4$ / sulfur	**17** 35.453 — (±1),3,5,7 / 238.6 / 172.17 / 3.214 — **Cl** / $[Ne]3s^23p^5$ / chlorine	**18** 39.948 — 0 / 87.5 / 84 / 1.7824 — **Ar** / $[Ne]3s^23p^6$ / argon
31 69.723 — 3 / 2477 / 302.93 / 5.907 — **Ga** / $[Ar]4s^23d^{10}4p^1$ / gallium	**32** 72.64 — 2,(4) / 3103 / 1210.6 / 5.323 — **Ge** / $[Ar]4s^23d^{10}4p^2$ / germanium	**33** 74.92160 — (±3),5 / 886 (sub.) / 1090 (28 bar) / 5.72 — **As** / $[Ar]4s^23d^{10}4p^3$ / arsenic	**34** 78.96 — -2,(4),6 / 958.1 / 490 / 4.79 — **Se** / $[Ar]4s^23d^{10}4p^4$ / selenium	**35** 79.904 — (±1),5 / 331.93 / 266 / 3.119 — **Br** / $[Ar]4s^23d^{10}4p^5$ / bromine	**36** 83.80 — 0 / 120.9 / 116.6 / 3.708 — **Kr** / $[Ar]4s^23d^{10}4p^6$ / krypton
49 114.818 — 3 / …3 / .76 — **In** / $[Kr]5s^24d^{10}5p^1$ / indium	**50** 118.71 — 2,(4) / 2875 / 505.12 / 7.30 — **Sn** / $[Kr]5s^24d^{10}5p^2$ / tin	**51** 121.76 — (±3),5 / 1860 / 903.89 / 6.684 — **Sb** / $[Kr]5s^24d^{10}5p^3$ / antimony	**52** 127.60 — -2,(4),6 / 1263.1 / 722.7 / 6.24 — **Te** / $[Kr]5s^24d^{10}5p^4$ / tellurium	**53** 126.90447 — (±1),5,7 / 457.35 (35 bar) / 387 / 4.93 — **I** / $[Kr]5s^24d^{10}5p^5$ / iodine	**54** 131.293 — 0 / 166.1 / 161.3 / 5.88 — **Xe** / $[Kr]5s^24d^{10}5p^6$ / xenon
204.3833 — (1),3	**82** 207.2 — (2),4	**83** 208.98038 — (3),5	**84** [208.9824] — 2,(4)	**85** [209.987] — (±1),3,5,7	**86** [222.017] — 0

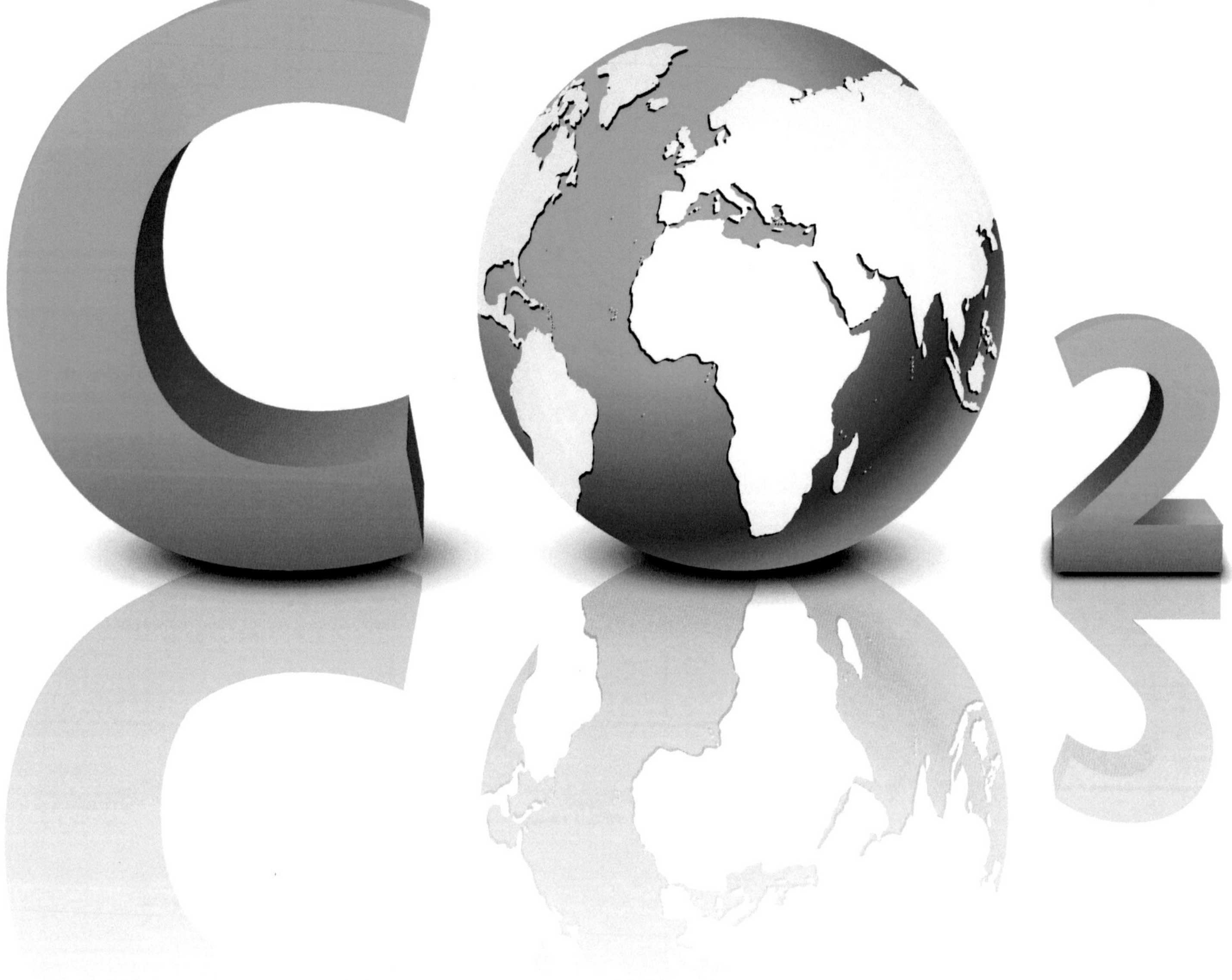

You can learn more by researching on the internet or by reaching out to your teachers, parents, and friends for additional information.

Visit

BABY PROFESSOR
EDUCATION KIDS

www.BabyProfessorBooks.com

to download Free Baby Professor eBooks and view
our catalog of new and exciting Children's Books

Made in the USA
Monee, IL
30 March 2022

93785595R00040